Tiger Talk

Learning the T Sound

Sharon Moore

Phonics
for the
REAL World™

Rosen Classroom Books and Materials™
New York

Tigers are orange and white.

Tigers have black stripes.

Tigers have big teeth.

Tigers have long tails.

Tigers have four toes.

Some tigers live where it is cold.

Some tigers live where it is hot.

Some tigers live in zoos.

Some tigers sit in tall grass.

Tiger cubs go with their mom.

Word List

tails

tall

teeth

tiger

toes

Instructional Guide

Note to Instructors:

One of the essential skills that enable a young child to read is the ability to associate letter-sound symbols and blend these sounds to form words. Phonics instruction can teach children a system that will help them decode unfamiliar words and, in turn, enhance their word-recognition skills. We offer a phonics-based series of books that are easy to read and understand. Each book pairs words and pictures that reinforce specific phonetic sounds in a logical sequence. Topics are based on curriculum goals appropriate for early readers in the areas of science, social studies, and health.

Letter/Sound: t – Briefly review beginning consonant **m** words from previous lessons. Display the words *Mom* and *Tom*. Talk about the initial **t** sound. Ask the child to tell how the words are the same and different. Continue with *make – take, map – tap, mop – top*. Have the child read and write the initial **t** words.

Phonics Activities: Ask the child to name time words that begin with **t** *(today, tomorrow, Tuesday, ten, two)*. Continue with action words, body parts, etc. List the words and have the child underline the initial **t** in each one.

- On a chalkboard or dry-erase board, write the following compound words beginning with **t**: *tablecloth, tablespoon, toothbrush, tiptoe, teapot, teaspoon, toolbox, tugboat*. Pronounce each word and have the child identify each separate word within the compound word *(table-cloth, tooth-brush, tea-pot,* etc.). Talk about how two short words have been combined to make one new word. Make or buy picture cards for each of the single words. Have the child combine the pictures to make compound words, matching them to the list. Have them underline the initial **t** in each word.

Additional Resources:
- Chancellor, Deborah. *Tiger Tales.* New York: DK Publishing, Inc., 2000.
- DuTemple, Lesley A. *Tigers.* Minneapolis, MN: The Lerner Publishing Group, 1996.
- Simon, Seymour. *Big Cats.* New York: HarperCollins Children's Books, 1991.
- Welsbacher, Anne. *Tigers.* Minneapolis, MN: ABDO Publishing Company, 2000.

Published in 2002 by The Rosen Publishing Group, Inc.
29 East 21st Street, New York, NY 10010

Copyright © 2002 by The Rosen Publishing Group, Inc.

Book Design: Haley Wilson

Photo Credits: Cover © Telegraph Colour Library/FPG International; p. 3 © Planet Earth Pictures/FPG International; p. 5 © Zig Leszczynski/Animals Animals; p. 7 © John Giustina/FPG International; p. 9 © Mark Stouffer/Animals Animals; p. 11 © David Boyle/Animals Animals; p. 13 © Lynn Stone/Animals Animals; p. 15 © Peter Weimann/Animals Animals; p. 17 © Richard Kolar/ Animals Animals; p. 19 © Robert Winslow/Animals Animals; p. 21 © VCG/ FPG International.

Library of Congress Cataloging-in-Publication Data

Moore, Sharon.
    Tiger talk: learning the T sound / Sharon Moore.—1st ed.
        p. cm.— (Power phonics/phonics for the real world)
    ISBN 0-8239-5914-7 (lib. bdg.)
    ISBN 0-8239-8259-9 (pbk.)
    6-pack ISBN 0-8239-9227-6
    1. Tigers—Juvenile literature. [1. Tigers.]   I. Title.
    II.Series.
    QL737.C23 M667 2001
    599.756—dc21
                                        00-013158

Manufactured in the United States of America